The Shape of a New Beginning

A true story about the struggle
between life, death & survival.

Agnes Takacs

Dedication

For my family, whose love has been the quiet strength
behind every page

Acknowledgment

To everyone who offered a kind word, a spark of inspiration, or a moment of support along the way, thank you.

About the Author

Born in Hungary, Agnes immigrated to Canada at just 15 with her mother and younger brother, beginning a life defined by courage, change, and starting over. By 18, she was married and soon became the proud mother of two children—a son and a daughter—building a family while learning what it means to persevere through every season of life.

At a time when many people settle into what is familiar, Agnes chose something braver: she left Canada and retired to Florida to finally make her dreams come true. In 2019, she became a United States citizen, a milestone that marked not an ending, but yet another new beginning.

Now 72, Agnes has lived a life shaped by reinvention—by the moments that force you to begin again, and the quiet determination it takes to keep moving forward. For years, she wrote stories privately, never publishing them, keeping her words close as if they belonged only to her.

Until now.

In this book, Agnes shares a story inspired by the truth she knows best: life can change from one day to the next, in an instant, without warning, and sometimes without mercy. But change can also bring unexpected strength, second chances, and the kind of hope you don't understand until you've had to rebuild.

This is her first time sharing her work with the public—an honest, heartfelt debut from a woman who has truly lived what she writes.

Prologue:
The Space Between Breaths

There is a moment—just before panic fully takes hold—when the mind goes strangely quiet.

It is not peace. It is not calm. It is something suspended in between.

That was where I lived for two days.

In that suspended space between fear and surrender, between consciousness and something else I still cannot fully name, I existed in fragments. I did not know if I was alive or already drifting toward death. Time stopped behaving the way it was supposed to. Minutes stretched into hours. Hours collapsed into nothing. Sounds felt distant, distorted, unreal. The walls of my own home felt unfamiliar, as if I had slipped into a version of reality where I did not quite belong.

My body was failing me, piece by piece, while my mind clung desperately to awareness. I could feel myself weakening, yet some instinct refused to let go. Something inside me stayed alert, watchful, waiting.

Looking back now, it feels like a horrific nightmare. But nightmares end when you wake up.

This one did not.

Contents

Chapter One:
The Accident That Never Left

The accident happened in 2019.

At the time, it didn't seem catastrophic. A car crash—sudden, violent, but survivable. I walked away with neck and back pain, shaken but upright. No broken bones. No hospital stay. No dramatic diagnosis that would have warned me what was coming.

I thought I was lucky.

What I did not understand then was that trauma does not always announce itself immediately. Sometimes it waits. Sometimes it settles quietly into your body, embedding itself into muscles and joints, slowly rewriting your relationship with pain.

Months passed.

At first, the discomfort was manageable. Then it began to grow. The pain took hold in my right pelvis—a deep, unrelenting ache that tightened its grip week after week. It wasn't sharp at first; it was heavy, persistent, impossible to ignore.

Walking became difficult. Standing became exhausting. Each step felt like a negotiation between willpower and agony. I learned to plan movements carefully, measuring distances, calculating how much pain each action would cost me.

At the time, I did not have medical insurance. Physical therapy was not an option. I tried what I could afford: a few chiropractic visits, occasional massage treatments. They brought brief relief, just enough to make me hopeful, but no real healing followed.

Eventually, I needed a cane.

That was the moment reality shifted. When you reach for a cane, not because it feels supportive, but because you cannot walk without it, something inside you breaks a little. It is a quiet breaking—no sound, no warning—just a sudden awareness that your body is no longer reliable.

Still, life continued. Or at least, I told myself it did.

Chapter Two:
The Morning Everything Changed

It was August 2024.

The morning began like any other. I woke early—around six a.m.—the house still quiet, the air heavy with that strange stillness that exists just before the day begins. The light filtering through the windows was soft, ordinary, unremarkable.

I swung my legs over the side of the bed, preparing to go to the bathroom.

That is when I slipped.

The tiles beneath my feet offered no mercy. My body went down hard, my right side taking the full force of the fall. The impact knocked the breath out of me. My head struck the tile—sharp, cold, unforgiving.

I did not lose consciousness.

In some ways, I wish I had.

Pain arrived instantly, flooding my body in waves. The kind of pain that steals your breath and leaves your thoughts scattered. I tried to orient myself, to assess the damage. My pelvis screamed. My knee throbbed. My head pulsed with each heartbeat.

I reached for the poster bed, gripping it with both hands, desperate to pull myself up.

I fell again.

This time, my knee struck the floor with a sickening impact that sent nausea through me. My body refused to cooperate. No matter how much I willed it, I could not stand. I could not climb back onto the bed.

That was when I realized something terrifying.

My cane was in the living room.

So was my phone.

Chapter Three:
Trapped

I lay on the bedroom floor, staring at the ceiling, trying to slow my breathing. Panic hovered just beneath the surface, waiting for permission to take over.

I told myself to stay calm.

Help would come later. I just needed to rest. Just for a little while.

I pulled the bedspread and blanket down from the bed and wrapped myself in them, lying on the cold tiles. The floor seeped into my bones. I tried to relax, convinced that if I could just let the pain settle, my body would cooperate again.

Instead, I grew weaker.

Time passed in uneven fragments. My muscles trembled. My mouth grew dry. The effort of simply staying awake became exhausting.

Eventually, through sheer determination, I began to crawl. Every movement sent sharp pain through my hip and knee, but I forced myself forward inch by inch until I reached the living room.

The sofa looked like salvation, but no matter how I tried, I could not get up onto it.

I sat on the floor beside it, thinking of solutions. Later, I lay down on the floor to rest.

The pain intensified.

My body shook with exhaustion. The sofa did not save me—it only reminded me how little strength I had left.

I was alone.

And the day was only beginning.

Chapter Four: Silence

As the hours passed, I tried to contact my family.

I found my phone and attempted to message my brother on WhatsApp. I didn't want to call my daughter while she was at work. I didn't want to alarm her over what I hoped was temporary.

The message never sent.

My phone battery died mid-sentence.

I turned to my laptop, hoping I could email someone instead. But that battery died too—unexpected, inexplicable. Both chargers were plugged in behind the sofa. When I tried to reach them, my elbow knocked the laptop off the table.

It hit the floor and broke.

The internet was gone.

The phone was dead.

I had no voice.

By the end of the day, my body ached in ways I didn't know were possible. Hunger gnawed at me, dull and persistent, but movement felt unbearable. I was lucky—there were grapes and a bottle of water on the side table. I rationed them carefully, aware I had no idea how long this would last.

That night, I slept—or maybe I passed out.

The line between the two blurred.

Chapter Five:
The Second Day

Morning came too soon.

I woke stiff and disoriented, my mouth dry and my thoughts foggy. My body felt heavier, less responsive, as though it no longer belonged to me. I crawled on my stomach toward the TV console, trying to reach the home phone resting in its holder, but it was too high. I tried using my cane to knock it down, straining with what little strength I had, but the phone would not fall to the floor. I could not reach it.

I crawled to the bathroom, needing to use the toilet, but I could not pull myself up. In that moment, stripped of dignity and strength, I peed on the blanket beneath me. I crawled back to the bedroom, pulled a dry blanket over myself, and tried to gather what little composure I had left.

Still hoping to sustain myself, I attempted to crawl to the refrigerator for bread and water, but I did not have the strength to open the door. That realization hurt more than the pain itself—something so simple should not have been impossible. More water bottles sat on the dining table. Using my cane, I managed to knock them down to the floor, grateful and ashamed at the same time.

Eventually, I crawled back to the living room and lay down on the carpet. I was weak. I was exhausted. As the day wore on, something inside me began to unravel.

I became delirious.

I heard voices outside the house—clear and distinct. People talking. Someone was asking if anyone had called an ambulance. Someone answering that nobody had. I saw lights that looked like emergency vehicles.

Hope surged through me, fragile and desperate.

But no one came.

Chapter Six:
The People in Green

In the afternoon, I sat on the floor near the window, drawn to the light.

That was when I saw her.

A woman stood outside my living room window, wearing what appeared to be a green uniform. My heart raced. She looked official—like someone from a wellness service, someone sent to check on me.

I banged on the window with my cane.

She turned, glanced in my direction, and looked away.

She did not care.

Later, a man in a similar green uniform joined her. I could hear them talking. I held my breath, convinced help was finally here.

They left.

That night, I thought I heard people near the back of the house, as if they were peering through the windows. Whether it was real or my mind betraying me, I still cannot say.

Chapter Seven:
The Third Day

On the third morning, around ten a.m., the woman returned.

She gestured toward my phone, as if trying to signal something. But the phone was dead. I could not respond. I could not call.

Again, she left.

By then, hunger and dehydration had hollowed me out. My chest began to ache. Panic finally took hold—not frantic, but heavy and suffocating. I thought this might be the end.

I refused to accept it.

Summoning the last of my strength, I crawled toward the side door leading to the garage. I repeatedly pressed the panic button on my car key, again and again, hoping someone would hear.

No one did.

After I managed to open the side door to the garage, I grabbed a mop and tried to reach the garage door opener, stretching upward with everything I had. It was too high. I didn't have the strength to reach it.

I crawled toward the side door leading outside, hoping I could open it. But I couldn't pull myself up high enough to reach the handle. Desperate, I tied the vacuum cord around the handle, hoping I could use it to pull myself upright.

Chapter Eight: Choosing Life

Something shifted inside me.

I was afraid—but I was not ready to die.

I forced myself onto my knees, falling back more times than I can count. Somehow, I reached the side door and pulled it open, collapsing into the garage.

I grabbed the mop, stretching it toward the garage door opener, but missed. Crawling again, I tied a vacuum cord around the door handle, using it as leverage to pull myself upright.

That was when I heard a voice.

"Where are you?"

I whispered, barely audible, "I'm at the side door."

The door opened.

A first responder stood there.

Help had finally arrived.

Chapter Nine:
After Survival

They took me to the hospital.

I was severely dehydrated, bruised from head to toe. I spent a week on a heart monitor. My hair was so tangled from dehydration it took two weeks to comb out.

When I looked in the mirror, I barely recognized myself.

The hospital food was awful, but I had a private room. Physical therapy consisted of slow walks down hallways, like a fragile animal relearning how to move.

My brother flew in from Canada. He visited me every day. He took care of me when I returned home.

He is the hero of this story.

Chapter Ten:
The Mystery That Remains

When I asked my neighbors if they had seen anyone in green uniforms, they all said no.

The woman behind my house mentioned seeing my bathroom light on for two nights.

I still believe those people were real.

The police report did not mention them.

The mystery remains.

Epilogue: Rebirth

Thanks to my hip surgeon, Dr. Super Cooper, I can walk again.

Healing took time—not just physically, but emotionally. Trauma lingers. Survival changes you.

This is a true story.

A story of survival.

Of near-death.

Of consciousness stretched to its limits.

And of choosing life—when death was very close.